# Common Sense Is Not That Common

## 11 powerful principles to a fuller, more meaningful, life

### by David Kottler

SMART BUSINESS® BOOKS
*An Imprint of Smart Business® Network Inc.*

Common Sense Is Not That Common
COPYRIGHT © 2016 David Kottler

Published by Smart Business Books
An imprint of Smart Business Network Inc.
835 Sharon Drive, Suite 200
Westlake, OH 44145

Printed in the United States of America
Editor: Dustin S. Klein
Cover and Interior Design: Randy Wood

ISBN: 978-0-9964080-8-0
Library of Congress Control Number: 2016940075

For my parents,
Barney Kottler and Lois Gray,
thank you for your spirit and generosity.

For my loving wife, Marcela.

# The Serenity Prayer

God grant me the serenity
To accept the things I cannot change;
Courage to change the things I can;
And wisdom to know the difference.

Living one day at a time;
Enjoying one moment at a time;
Accepting hardships as the pathway to
peace;
Taking, as He did, this sinful world
As it is, not as I would have it;
Trusting that He will make all things right
If I surrender to His will;
So that I may be reasonably happy in this life
And supremely happy with Him
Forever and ever in the next.

Amen

# Contents

# Preface

*Dad's story: How three simple words wiped away 45 years of miscommunication and frustration*

My dad and I worked together for more than 20 years. We were both independent, strong-willed individuals, which led to many conflicts during those years. However, I was taught to respect him as my elder, as well as my father. In a letter I wrote to him in 1993, less than three months before his ultimately fatal stroke, I stated:

*The practical experience and wisdom you gained became very valuable lessons for me and helped me form my ideals and insights.*

*We did have a lot of conflict. Conflict led to independence. Independence led to me trying my own path, but with an appreciation for the opportunity and wisdom I got from you.*

*I have no regrets over my choices, and am gratified that the conflict forced me my own way, which eventually led to greater self-esteem and my own failures.*

*It was this sense of self and overcoming failures that afforded me a much greater appreciation of your efforts, your successes and your failures.*

*You have helped me grow as a son, as a father and as a business person.*

Unlike many people, I was very fortunate in my relationship with my dad. I truly loved him, and found him to be a source of a great deal of wisdom, as well as solace in difficult times. My father was famous for his sayings—bits of wisdom he gleaned from what he read, his studies and his ancestors. Mostly, they came from his life experiences. He also liked to remind me, "Good judgment comes from experience; unfortunately, experience comes from bad judgment."

This book is dedicated to him—his ideals and life values, which helped shape my attitudes and core values in life, as well as my appreciation for all that life is and can be. Throughout, I include anecdotes from my life as well as from our life together—all of which are aimed to further illustrate the impact of his nuggets of wisdom and humor.

With all the conflict, frustration and sibling rivalry (for our dad's money and affection) impinging on my relationship with my dad, it is no wonder that I knew the meaning of a love/hate relationship. I'm sure this apparent ambiguity was prompted by our own feelings of inadequacy, or even uncertainty in our parent's love for us. However, all this was transformed into pure love when I experienced my dad's deathbed expressions of love for me.

My father endured a massive stroke one morning in the winter of 1993. After receiving a phone call from the housekeeper, I rushed to the house filled with trepidation. Ten minutes later, I met the emergency vehicle there. Dad was conscious. He was actually joking as they lifted him from the bed and told the medics to "roll me over in the clover" as they shifted his position.

After they took him to the hospital, I found myself looking in his closet and was struck with a profound sense of sadness and respect for his shunning of material things. He had a very modest wardrobe and a single pair of beat-up shoes. At that moment, I realized how much Dad lived his values of moderation and put the family first by denying himself the many luxuries he could have had.

I was motivated to make an audiotape describing the love and admiration I felt for him, which I planned to take to the hospital so that he could listen to it in what I believed might be his final hours. I made the tape and hooked it up to automatically play over and over.

The next morning, the family gathered at the hospital to visit my father. As we walked toward his room, a nurse met us in the hallway.

"Which one of you is David?" She asked, a grave look on her face.

"I am."

She proceeded to tell me that my father, in his final lucid words, strained to say, "Tell David I love him."

This simple statement transformed more than 40 years of conflict and fighting into pure love for my father. I realized that not only did Dad love me dearly, but he only had my best intentions in mind at all times.

It is my hope that as you read this book, you'll find guidance, humor, and comfort from the insights my father imparted to me, just as I did.

David Kottler
Cleveland, Ohio
June 2016

*Author's Note*: In several places in the text, you will see references to G-d. I chose this because we honor the Lord's name by not writing it fully.

# *Chapter 1*

*"Common sense is not that common."*

My father had an experience during my lifetime in which he entered into a joint venture with a farmer to further what he thought were their mutual interests. Dad was an innovator, and when he moved the family business into the realm of egg buying and distribution, he saw the advantages of setting up his own supply chain by partnering with a farmer to establish an egg farm—years before this became the model of the industry.

He and the farmer pledged money and assets. The farmer even put up his farm to help secure the operating capital. Unfortunately, they were not well enough capitalized against early losses. The egg market was so depressed that first year the selling price ended up lower than the cost of producing eggs. To my father's amazement, the farmer was caught unprepared. He lost his farm, and they lost the business.

Looking back at it, this is a prime example of the farmer not using simple common sense. Some type of collaboration that was predetermined by the two men could have saved the enterprise. The farmer, putting everything on the line with no backup plan, over leveraged himself without telling my father that he'd gone all-in. My father, thinking the farmer using his farm as collateral meant the farmer was committed to the project, gained a false sense of security that the farmer knew what he was doing. He did not foresee the market falling apart. Had they spent time discussing the potential ups and downs of the egg market, they might have used better judgment—either my father choosing a better business partner or the farmer making sure he was adequately capitalized to sustain a slower build-up of the business.

Every day we are inundated with information from a variety of sources. Our natural reaction is to shut out as much as possible to avoid overload. So how do we get the good information, which helps us make good decisions, and keep out the bad? How do we learn to look under the hood or behind the curtain to get at the truth of the situation? These are not easy things to accomplish but certainly critically important in determining the outcome.

It is necessary to develop a capacity for looking at things from as wide a perspective as possible. Don't be afraid to get a coach. Don't be afraid to interact with others who may have more experience than you and who have been successful. Try to understand where the other person is coming from. If there is truly a win-win opportunity presented, pursue it. If any deal is one-sided, it is not sustainable. In fact, if both parties are not truly benefiting from the relationship or partnership, why would they stay engaged? We're hardwired to be social and competitive, but with a better awareness of both sides of the equation we're able to achieve a better outcome.

Common sense also comes into play when analyzing opportunities presented to you. If something sounds too good to be true, it usually is. My father warned that you must take everything with a grain of salt and look at things from a very pragmatic standpoint. He counseled that you should consider all the features of the deal and the motivations of all parties concerned to ensure there is truly win-win potential where all parties concerned have a common goal and skin in the game. It's important that no one involved suggests that the other person is going to get something for nothing, because that is a huge red flag.

In my own life, I have made several large business errors from which I have learned the truth of the adage "unfortunately, good judgment comes out of bad." I came into my father's food distribution business as a way to put myself through law school. My childhood dream was to become an attorney. I had no interest in joining my dad's business because it did not look very appealing from the outside. Dad was a great survivalist and had outlasted other family members by purchasing their shares of the business or watching them leave the company. He eventually became the sole owner. He was self-sufficient and not in debt, the family business gratefully was the source of basic food, clothing, and shelter for our family. However, there were no luxuries—we learned the difference between wants and needs.

When I joined him, the business was languishing at around $500,000 in sales, without much prospect for growth. It was stalled due to many factors: my parents' divorce, a lack of focus, and an uncomfortable relationship between my dad and his brother—who remained in the company but not as an owner.

My father reluctantly gave me a job at the age of 22 for a starting salary of $600 per month so I could earn enough to attend law school at night. Over the next five years, I was fortunate to earn an excellent legal education and to pass the bar. At the same time, my day job became very productive and, to my great surprise, fun.

At the end of five years, our business had grown tenfold to around $5 million a year; and so did my salary. I also rewarded my father by implementing some beneficial retirement benefits for him as gratitude for his hard work and the sacrifices he'd made. I did not like the idea of being in the commodity business, where you had to fight for every single penny. Instead, what was fun for me was seeking out products that were of great value to the consumers, which allowed me to develop exclusive relationships with the manufacturers. As our company grew, my responsibility was to find, market and distribute these types of products.

My first great find was Häagen-Dazs ice cream, which back in 1977 had very limited distribution. When I saw it advertised in the Neiman Marcus Christmas catalogue for some outrageous amount of money, I liked what I saw and believed this was a product with real panache.

I flew to New York to meet with the owner, Reuben Mattus. We made a handshake deal, which lasted many years. That ended some years after Pillsbury bought the company from Mattus for $70 million in 1983. This made me realize that who you are doing business with is the greatest single determinant of longevity—not a contract.

Our business continued to grow with the usual ups and downs. By 1993 I found myself at a crossroads. I had just finished an expensive and time-consuming divorce. Our business consisted of various niche ice cream and bakery products, which were lucrative and enjoyed good distribution but had limited sales revenue potential. I was ready to expand the business again, which in retrospect was the beginning of the end.

At that time, Ben and Jerry's, Dove Bars and related products, Good Humor ice cream novelties, Healthy Choice ice cream, and Häagen-Dazs all shared one characteristic: corporate marketing dollars. Essentially, I did not need to invest any of our company's money into marketing. Either the manufacturer paid the bill, word-of-mouth drove sales, or the product had very strong repeat purchase power.

I determined the next logical step was to invest in carrying a more mainstream product that allowed the company to earn less per sale but resulted in higher consumption and increased volume sales. That led us to acquire a half-gallon, high-quality ice cream line, which required a significant investment by the company. Unlike the premium products, we had to come up with a third of the marketing dollars required to promote the products.

After evaluating numerous options, I selected Edy's/Dreyer's. It had an excellent reputation for successfully marketing and distributing its products nationally, but had a less-than-stellar reputation for how they treated some of their distribution relationships. Several friends of mine had lost their business through financial loss or lawsuit, so the warning signs were there.

Despite this, my desire to get into the big leagues of ice cream distribution won out. We signed an agreement with Edy's. And while we distributed millions of dollars of Edy's in the market, unfortunately we lost money on every gallon we distributed. We had incorrectly calculated on a percentage basis that we could make some money. No one had the common sense to see if the actual cost of distributing this product would be profitable. Because the selling price of each gallon was so much lower than what we were used to, our estimates were ill-informed.

As a result, after two years, we owed Edy's $1 million for our past purchases and its promise to fund us so long as we were successfully penetrating the market came to a screeching halt. The adage "if it sounds too good to be true" rang very sharply in my ears.

Unfortunately, my common sense meter was not operating very well when I entered into the Edy's deal. Why I thought they would treat me differently than my friends who had lost their businesses was beyond me. I should have known much better.

The same year I lost my business, 17 other Edy's distributors lost theirs—so it's pretty safe to assume the problem was likely more on their end than the distributors.

This was an expensive lesson, one which I obviously have never forgotten. In fact, it served as the impetus of my deeply held belief of the importance of increasing philanthropy, which was something I became more involved with during our business's glory years. As Dad always said, "It's better to give than receive."

By being aware of your intentions—as well as those of the people with whom you want to develop business relationships—you're one step closer to being successful. When you are honest and transparent with others, you should always expect the same from them. That doesn't preclude you from doing your homework before making a major decision, but it can allow you to take a more holistic view of the situation. And finally, don't underestimate the importance of talking to people who you can trust and have the experience you may need to tap into to further mutual goals.

The bottom line is that common sense needs to be the bedrock on which all your decisions are made. Always look at things from a pragmatic viewpoint, with a clear eye toward all possible realities. Remember that no one is infallible, but by adhering to these tactics and principles you will increase your odds of being successful.

As my mother's favorite cousin Alvin Gray would often say, "If I'm right 51 percent of the time, I'm ahead of the game!"

### *Principle*

Good judgment comes from experience; unfortunately, experience comes from bad judgment.

# Chapter 2

*"That's why they put erasers on pencils."*

*"Just do the best you can."*

*"Everyone stumbles. It's what you do after that that counts."*

My father was a difficult taskmaster. He always said he was just trying to instill qualities within me that would stay with me for the rest of my life. Sometimes, it got to be a bit much. All I really wanted were some words of support and encouragement rather than criticism or the constant pushing me to do more. However, the nice thing was that whenever I would complain about that, my father would switch gears, praise my efforts, and become a source of warmth and support.

His saying, "Just do the best you can," probably resonates the most with me among everything he ever said, as long as I'm being honest with myself about what comprises "the best." This is a principle I am constantly trying to impress upon my children because I think it is such a source of comfort and direction in trying times.

Dad's advice goes with another one of his sayings, "Done is better than perfect." Together, they are designed to motivate each of us to put forth our best efforts and to be satisfied with those efforts, regardless of the consequences. I take my father's advice to heart, knowing it does not take away my goals or desire to succeed at whatever I put my mind to, but rather to not become discouraged along the path.

My wife and I had a recent opportunity to impress this concept upon our teenage daughter. She had been struggling with school in her efforts to achieve straight-A's in her 10th-grade classes. She works hard and consistently outperforms her native ability, but this comes at tremendous personal cost—being anxious most of the time. She is anxious about her studying and putting in many more hours than normal, as well as the results of her grades. This anxiety got to the point where she was totally overwhelmed at finals time, swimming in a sea of papers in her room that she could not get organized to study.

My wife was very concerned for our daughter's health. She reached out to the school and asked what could be done to alleviate the overwhelming stress and anxiety. They were kind, and responded that our daughter could be excused from the finals and get a pass grade for the semester because her grade to that point was more than 100 percent in all of her classes.

This sounded very appealing when we first heard it because it addressed her immediate discomfort. But when the actual report card came and our daughter realized all her hard work for the 16-week semester was not given any specific credit other than a pass grade, she really wanted to take on the challenge of taking her finals and getting a grade for her efforts.

Thankfully, the school was agreeable—so long as Ariela could demonstrate that she was not overwhelmed by her studies or anxiety over grades and could handle these types of situations in the future. We were very pleased, and Ariela felt a great relief that we had heard her, were supportive of her just doing her best, and that the process instilled in her the importance of grit—of not giving up.

There are many business books out there about the power of grit and persistence. There is also a great YouTube video of a TED Talk given by Angela Lee Duckworth, which has more than 1.5 million hits. Duckworth wrote a book called "The Key to Success? Grit." In it, she identified that the one common characteristic of children in being able to predict their future success was not ability or IQ, but rather grit—the power to keep trying and be persistent in one's goals.

Grit is a wonderful trait. It is a powerful aid that helps children develop the resilience and determination necessary to rise from the ashes and get up when life's inevitable stumbles come along. In my life, I've had quite a few stumbles that led to my learning and ultimate belief in these principles.

When I was losing my business, I became very depressed. My career had become very important to me—not just for the financial benefits I enjoyed, but for the feeling of success that became a part of my persona. The business was, in a sense, my baby. I still had a great respect and gratitude for the start I got in life due to my father and grandmother's efforts many years before. But I had so many insecurities of what I would be able to do for a job. There were concerns about the fact that I had become very accustomed to having many employees who handled much of the daily work for me while my job had been to find new products, manage those relationships, and monitor and guide the sales process. The thought of being on my own—and doing everything myself—was very scary.

I was also terribly troubled, feeling I had let my current family down. I felt as if I was letting my ancestors down by having their legacy, this business which had persisted, get taken over by a creditor. Add to this an overwhelming concern for my employees, of whom I was so fond and felt a paternal sense of obligation.

At the time, my sister Kathy told me, "If it doesn't kill you, it will make you stronger." That sounded comforting, but I simply could not see the light at the end of the tunnel nor have a picture or vision of what my life would look like without the business.

As if the business concerns weren't enough, within the same year I also lost my father to a stroke and was getting divorced for the second time, having failed in that marriage attempt.

Reflecting upon my dad's words, "When you're having problems, pretend like you are floating on your back" and "Go to sleep and sometimes the answers will come to you in your sleep" were of some help, but the real answer was finding my faith in G-d, understanding that he put me here for a purpose, and I had that obligation to fulfill it. This sense of responsibility and desire to help others, as well as find a way to fulfill my mission of trying to increase philanthropy, became the energy and motivation needed to activate my grit. This enabled me to get through these very dark days.

Later, my grit played another role—helping me seek out and fulfill my desire to establish a happy family with a loving wife. Today, I feel so blessed and grateful for having gone through this process and hitting rock bottom.

I believe the trick in surviving difficult situations is to look at the challenges as opportunities for growth. If you do so, you convert the bad adrenaline or cortisol, which causes stress, to more productive internal change. You learn how to acknowledge the feelings. Instead of viewing the situation as stressful, you begin to look at it as a challenge you are happy to try to meet. And, you grow in the process.

When Thomas Edison was chastised about his many failures in his quest to invent the electric bulb, he wonderfully said, "These were not failures, but rather each was a successful effort in showing me what would not work." This is a wonderful lesson for life.

I once heard a story about a family who each week at the dinner table celebrated their failures. They went around the table and each person shared what it was that they failed at that week. This is an incredibly powerful exercise. It instills a sense of creativity and a willingness to strive for new ideas and solutions to challenges because failure is celebrated for making the effort rather than for the failing itself.

This family's tradition fits nicely with the principle of doing the best you can and not being overly concerned about the results: If you have the grit to keep moving, you ultimately will fulfill your goals. At the end of the day, people are generally much more remorseful about the things they did not attempt in life rather than the things they tried.

## *Principle*

Be resilient. Acknowledge your mistakes, embrace failure, and know that it's a necessary step toward success.

# Chapter 3

*"To thine own self be true."*

My dad often quoted Shakespeare. Among his favorite bard sayings was, "To thine own self be true." It took me until much later in life to understand how important this simple philosophy was. In fact, it's a prime example of how wisdom can be so deep in its simplicity that it takes a certain advanced level of maturity to really absorb its meaning.

I must admit, I'm not completely sure what this saying actually meant to my father because we never discussed it. But I wish we had because the older I got, the more it meant to me. Perhaps this philosophy served as a guiding light for my father to try to live up to the ideals he espoused, even recognizing that life or circumstances put him in conflict with those ideals at times. Maybe it allowed him to forgive himself for those transgressions and still maintain a fervent belief in those ideals. Whatever the reason, the depth of Dad's wisdom through his sayings brings to mind a vision of digging into the earth with a shovel, searching for treasure and unearthing richness. But what's found is more than a material richness of money or treasure. Instead, it's a richness and fertility discovered through the depth of experience. So for me, this was really about digging beyond the past for ancient truth and wisdom.

In recent years, as I have become more involved in coaching programs that encourage us to be the best we can be and continually try to improve ourselves through learning, reading and sharing messages, I've discovered more wisdom. I am fascinated by people, their behavior and the books they write, and incorporate new thinking into how I see the world—and, more importantly, myself.

One of the highlights of my youth occurred when I was in the third grade. I read a mystery book and had to present a report to my class. I shared enough details to pique my classmate's interest, but did not divulge the ending as I wanted them to read the book themselves and enjoy it. It was very gratifying and exhilarating for me to get swamped by my classmates after the school break, demanding more information about the book and telling me how interested they were. That's an experience that has stuck with me for decades.

These days, I've continued to absorb what I read. Numerous books have had a profound impact on helping me know myself better. The most interesting books are those that delve into the human psyche with a combination of stories to illustrate the points using real-life examples and science and behavioral testing results to back up the hypotheses.

Two of my favorites are Sally Hogshead's, "Fascinate: How to Make Your Brand Impossible to Resist," and Charles Duhigg's, "Smarter, Faster, Better: The Secrets of Being Productive in Life and Business." What I have learned is that the better I know myself and why I do things, the more productive I become. Sally's book and website are incredibly insightful tools that help us see ourselves as the world sees us. In the process, we become more authentic and fascinating to our spouses, co-workers, families, business clients and associates. Her method helps people become more of who they already are—which was the underlying message of what my father tried to impart to me through the master poet's words.

Charles' book provides the reader stories and examples of how certain key principles have resulted in astounding successes, for example, the movie "Frozen." This has special meaning to me because "Let it Go" was one of my daughter Chaya Sara's favorite songs. She used to make me play it in the car each day as I drove her to school.

As Charles tells the story, apparently 18 months before the movie was released, the team developing it was in a terrible bind. They were stuck without a common theme that made sense and resonated with the test audience. But they found a solution and went on to release one of the most successful movies of all time.

The solution is akin to what a scientist studying diversity of plant and sea life in Australia learned. He discovered a much greater diversity of plant and sea life in areas where there had been a disruption of the environment—not too great and not too insignificant. But when a little extra light shone through the water and natural canopy covering, it allowed many other types of life to grow and thrive. This was much different than the areas where there was no disruption. In effect, it became survival of the fittest in the untouched areas, which resulted in much less diversity.

So the managers at Disney promoted a writer who was already on the project as co-director to take charge and change the situation. This small change forced the writer to take a more active role in managing the process and to listen more closely to all of her co-writers and others involved in the process.

The end result was solving the problem they had of being unable to find the mission or underlying message that held together the movie. Ultimately, it became one of how love can conquer fear. And it resulted in a movie that deeply inspired and entertained so many people in the true Disney fashion. It also serves as an excellent example of why it's important to know who you are and to strive to be that person.

## *Principle*

Know yourself and be yourself.

# Chapter 4

*"It's better to give than to receive."*

learned from my parents at a very early age that it's better to give than to receive. Inspiring stories abounded from both sides of the family describing how wealthier relatives would help less fortunate ones. My mother often regaled me with stories of how her father, a successful dentist, would help his siblings. They would visit often, sometimes weekly, for emotional and monetary support. Hearing these stories instilled in me a great sense of family and generosity.

I was also fortunate to develop a lifelong friendship and professional relationship with my mother's first cousin, Alvin. He became one of my role models for being philanthropic and active in good causes. Alvin probably gave many millions of dollars to his varied and favorite causes during his life, which turned out to be more money than he ended up with. This truly enriched his life, as well as the others who benefited from his largesse, and meant far more than the eventual wealth he could have kept for himself.

One Mother's Day, when I was 10 or 11 years old, I had a few dollars in my pocket that I had earned working at my dad's warehouse. The money was burning a hole in my pocket, so I went to the local drugstore to spend it. At the time, my favorite purchases were candy, comic books (I loved Superman and Batman), and the special bubblegum they sold in these containers where if you got the "multicolored" one you got a free drink at the soda fountain.

As I walked through the drugstore, I saw a beautiful box of candy that I thought my mother would appreciate. Without hesitation I decided to give up my treats and splurge on this Mother's Day present for my mom.

When I got home, I gave my mother the present. The look on her face—surprised delight—was well worth the cost of not buying the garbage I often did. The wonderful warmth I felt inside gave me a bodily confirmation of what my heart and head were telling me. It really impressed upon me at that early age the certainty that it was better to give than receive.

My wife and I often discuss the powerful imprints children receive at early ages, and how these imprints can be beneficial or harmful for many years to come. We understand the importance of these lessons, and the power of what imparting—

or instilling—them in youngsters can have. There is a saying that it's easier to write on a fresh piece of paper than one which has been written over many times. We are conscious of how important it is to live a value-driven life, so we try to incorporate a positive message or set good examples with everything we do because we recognize how deeply those messages stay with children for the rest of their lives. It's one of the things that amazes me about my wife—she is such an incredible mother who embodies the nurturing culture of Argentinian families—where she was born—and has raised her six daughters in an exemplary fashion.

Years later, when I was achieving success in my dad's business, I began going to Jewish Federation meetings. They would solicit and announce gifts to the annual campaign, and it was an eye-opening experience to learn the concept of *tzedakah* up close. In Hebrew, the word *tzedakah* does not mean charity or philanthropy, but literally means "justice or righteousness," and in traditional Judaism refers to the religious obligation to do what is right and just. In other words, we each have an obligation to help support our less-fortunate brethren, which puts giving in a totally different perspective. I attended several fundraising dinners where people would proudly—and publicly—announce their annual pledges to generate more enthusiasm for the process and probably generate a little peer pressure to achieve better results. You would swallow, take a deep breath, and perhaps make a pledge that seemed uncomfortably large but "felt good" because you knew it was for a good cause.

As I became more involved with Jewish orthodoxy and regularly studied the Torah, I learned there are actually eight levels of giving—the highest being to help someone become self-sufficient and enable them to stand on their own two feet. The irony is that this was one of my dad's favorite sayings!

According to Jewish philosopher Moses Maimonides, the levels are:

- **Level Eight**: Giving grudgingly, with a sour countenance.
- **Level Seven**: Giving less than you can afford, but doing so pleasantly.
- **Level Six**: Giving generously, but only after being asked.
- **Level Five**: Giving before you are asked.
- **Level Four**: The recipient knows the giver, but the giver does not know the recipient.
- **Level Three**: The giver knows the recipient, but the recipient does not know the giver.
- **Level Two**: Giving anonymously, where the recipient does not know the giver and vice versa.
- **Level One**: Helping someone become self-sufficient.

This really captures the old adage that it is better to "teach a man how to fish, than give him a fish." By doing so, it enables an individual to feel good about being able to stand on his own two feet, which was my father's most fervent desire for his children. Dad believed this was the most important lesson he could teach us. And I can attest to the fact that those lessons were not easy or always welcome, but they were lessons I look back on and am very grateful to have learned.

Certainly, any giving is desirable, but giving without your ego involved is doing so at a very high level. I learned recently—and the concept resonated with me strongly—that G-d does not care about the amount of money you give to charity or the sacrifices you make for him, but rather whatever it is that you do be done with a full and loving heart. It's amazing to think about how important attitude is in everything we do.

Why is giving so important and something that should be incorporated into your daily life? The reasons are many, and there are so many books available which measure the actual bodily and mental benefits that giving provides the giver. One study demonstrated that for every $100 worth of charity the donor gave, it resulted in additional income of almost $400 specifically related to that giving. This financial benefit pales in comparison to the mental and spiritual health benefits that researchers have discovered.

Tom Rath, considered one of the greatest thinkers of our time, in his most recent book wrote that having meaning in our lives is one of the three central components to being "fully charged." In Rath's work, meaning is actually equated with giving in some form or another. Countless studies have been done by psychologists, social psychologists and others to buttress this claim.

When I had the terrible misfortune of losing my business, my dad and my second marriage all in the same year, I was pretty devastated. Intuitively, I knew that some type of activity involved in trying to increase philanthropy could be the catalyst to get me back to the path I had envisioned for myself from an early age. My second career choice was influenced by my CPA, who suggested my legal background, my business and marketing background, and the network of advisers and other successful business owners I knew, could be good assets for a financial planning career.

The other attraction to this type of career path was I did not need a large amount of money or personnel to get started. The *why* I wanted to do it, aside from the more mundane aspects, was the opportunity to give my life more meaning by fulfilling a desire to help increase philanthropy. My goal was to utilize tax and estate planning concepts, as well as life insurance, to help people understand that it was possible to disinherit Uncle Sam and actually have more money for their families, favorite causes and charities.

Most people agree with the philosophy that it is better to give than to receive, but often don't know how to begin or where to put their efforts. I looked at my opportunity as an obligation to help demonstrate to clients or their advisers that perhaps they have enough assets to make contributions. Many times, these gifts can be made in a manner which helps the donor as well—from both a tax and financial standpoint.

Here in the U.S., we are blessed to have charitable planning concepts developed by the government called *split interest gifts*. Say what you want about the government, but it did realize that it was desirable to have private funding help many organizations, and that this type of giving can be many times more effective than just paying all those dollars as taxes. Certainly, those types of gifts versus taxes can help families accomplish much more on a specifically directed basis than by simply paying taxes.

Early in this new career, I remember presenting this idea to a potential client about how the estate tax was a totally voluntary tax because there were methods available to eliminate it as well as to reduce income taxes. The donor was shocked. He had never heard this from his advisers and was delighted that such a thing could be true. Since then, I've learned there are many reasons why advisers may not bring up the topic with their clients: It could be an area of practice with which they are not overly familiar or an expert. They might be concerned about offending their clients if they were seen as pushing them to give away money. However, when you can impart this message with the right attitude, and perhaps a story, or better yet a question to the donor—such as, "Could you please tell me of some occasions when you have been able to help others and how did that make you feel?"—it makes the conversation, and option, so much more personal.

There is a remarkable TED Talk Simon Sinek gave called "Start With Why." In it, Sinek discusses that "why" we do things is much more resonant with people than anything else. My *why* for wanting to become involved with financial planning was to help people increase their philanthropic efforts. If you ask people why they want to accumulate money, after they mention their personal and family needs, the next reason is that they want to have an impact on the world. What better way to do so than through effective charitable planning?

This is one of those big questions that we can all ask ourselves: How can we add meaning in our lives?

Not surprisingly, the answer is giving.

## *Principle*

The meaningful life is one that embodies a spirit of generosity.

# Chapter 5

*"Walk with your feet on the ground
and your head in the sky."*

*"Money is just a tool."*

When I was growing up, my great Uncle Henry Gray was considered the most successful of our living relatives. Henry was a self-made man who never received a formal education. He started working as a teenager in the drugstore industry for the Weinbergers, who owned a small but growing chain of local drug stores in Cleveland. Henry rose to an executive position and became invaluable to the organization, so much so that when it was time for them to expand nationally in 1945, they wanted to use his name, Gray, for the name of the chain. Thus, Gray Drug Stores Inc. was born. At age 65, Henry was mandated to retired, but he didn't retire from the industry. Instead, he joined another growing company and became the vice chairman of Revco, helping to oversee the organization's growth from $70 million to more than $2 billion.

One of Henry's favorite sayings was "Kiss a dollar bill and it won't kiss you back." He and his wife Ruth were the most generous people and never had children. They lavishly spent on their family and helped out whenever and wherever they could. Henry truly exemplified the concept that money is just a tool. He was known for giving children freshly minted dollar bills from a big wad he carried around with him, and offering up his sage advice about not kissing it. What a wonderful human being!

This lesson is one that took me nearly half a century to embrace. It took quite a while to look at the *why* I do what I do for a living and to try to add more meaning to my life. It also coincided with my introduction to Jewish orthodoxy and Torah study as a means to make my life more fulfilling and to add a sense of purpose. It is common wisdom that people often come to consider the fact there may be a higher power or creator of the universe when they have life issues forcing them to increase their faith or to look for answers that may not be readily apparent. I was no different.

The year was 1993, and I guess you could say my 45th year of life was a bad year by most standards. I lost a very valuable business, my father to a stroke, and initiated divorce proceedings for the second time in my life. It was my own personal triple whammy, and it forced me to reflect upon where I had been and my life goals. Here I was, looking back at my early 20s, when I'd been full of vim, vigor and hope—a young man starting out in life. And now, in my mid-40s, I was starting out again in a new career without the stability and love of an intact marriage, nor a happy home to raise my children together with their mother, which had always been my goal.

In my 20s, I was consumed with building the family business and enjoying the fruits of my labors with my family. I wanted to enjoy the proceeds of my hard work, maybe because I saw my father did not—and I believe this aged him. Perhaps it was just one of those contradictions that Dad had, where he said, "Money is just a tool" but never really enjoyed spending it—other than on many delightful family gatherings at restaurants. Instead, Dad kept saving his money because he never knew when it would be in short supply again, just like when he was a youngster.

But not me. I took my then three children— Jeremy, Zachary and Ashley—on vacations galore. We had a wonderful timeshare in Hilton Head that the whole family loved.

When that family broke up, it became much easier for me to understand Dad's philosophy surrounding money and recognize that there are more important values in life rather than how you spend your cash.

The Lord works in mysterious ways—that's for sure. And maybe, once our hearts are broken to some degree we make room for him to enter. At that point, things happen by some type of Divine Providence. This is a belief that I have come to embrace: That there is a G-d. He created the world. He cares deeply about us. And he watches over every step of our lives.

I had been working in my new career as a financial adviser for about a year when a new client suggested I meet him at an office that ironically was located inside my office building to pick up his documents for review at what he called a "lunch and learn." I had no idea what "lunch and learn" meant, but I was happy to meet him and get started on his case.

To my great surprise, the "learn" aspect of the lunch was a rabbi teaching Torah concepts to a group of around 35 people, 10 of whom I already knew. I must admit, I was somewhat shocked that all these people who I never considered religious, were actually meeting to learn and hear about the Torah. It was a real culture shock to me because I always considered myself *au courant* with ideas or movements. Yet, here were people I played golf and socialized with involved in the study of something of which I had almost zero knowledge.

The "lunch and learn" was mildly interesting, but the impact of seeing my contemporaries involved resonated deeper. And subsequently, when I was on an overnight trip with my then 13-year-old son and some other friends in our Indian Guides group, I had a chance to explore the conversation further. We were roused in the middle of the night by some ravenous raccoons. After we fended them off, we got into a campfire discussion about whom they studied with and recommended.

My interest was piqued. A few days later I went to another "lunch and learn" with a much smaller group—four people, three of whom I knew.

The rabbi leading the group asked if I would come to a *Shabbaton* the following weekend. I had never experienced a *Shabbos* before, but was game to try it.

What a remarkable experience it was. The idea is that we totally rest on *Shabbos* from dusk on Friday until sunset on Saturday, and spend the day in acknowledgment that G-d created the world, he provides for all our needs, and he rested on the Seventh Day. It reinforces the principal that money is just a tool and there is much more to life than its accumulation. I came away from it believing that the Torah could only have come from a higher being. My thought process was straightforward: If I believe that to be true, it was incumbent upon me to learn more about it and to start following the Torah as my ancestors had done for the past 3,000 years or so.

One thing led to another and I was hooked. One of the core benefits I found in each of the observant homes that I started to spend a part of each *Shabbos* in was the concept of a day of rest. The *Shabbat* was a time for family to enjoy and get together; to eat, to sing and to separate from the rest of the week by refraining from work, phone calls, texts, emails and other life distractions in order to focus on themselves and their families. This was a cherished goal I held for years—ever since realizing it was something I lacked growing up as a child and, unfortunately, during my first two marriages.

A year later, my rabbi and his wife suggested I might find a *Shabbaton* in Crown Heights enjoyable. A heavily Jewish neighborhood in Brooklyn, New York, Crown Heights was the epicenter of the *Chabad* movement—a movement of tremendous growth and success in helping Jewish people find their attachment to their roots.

*Chabad* employs a user-friendly manner for people to explore their Judaism without pressure to become religious. Rather, they lead by example and help facilitate one's Jewish *neshoma*, or soul, by stimulating them with Torah study. The movement grew by leaps and bounds. It was so successful that it could honestly be found wherever Coca-Cola was found, having expanded in the 1950s from a few dozen centers to more than 4,500 *Chabad* centers around the world today.

What a culture shock it was for me. But those in the movement are very experienced and adept at meeting Jewish people who have little or no orthodox background. They welcome them as fellow Jews, regardless of their lack of observance. This open-minded interaction is an aspect of the movement that I feel has made them successful at attracting new constituents. Some of those people become more observant, others become fully observant, and many just enjoy the interaction and never change their individual brand of Judaism.

Imagine an environment where you have full-fledged orthodox rabbis and people dressed in their black hats and religious garb mingling with business people, their wives and families, each coming from different degrees of wealth, sophistication, and religious observance. Somehow, it works.

There were approximately 150 attendees at the *Shabbaton* I attended—men and women from quite literally around the world. They came to explore, to hear the brilliant keynote lecturer who spoke on Jewish Meditation, and to meet people—perhaps like me, in the hopes of finding a partner who would want to grow and consider starting a family while incorporating the "*Chabad* style" into our new life.

The social setting is not like the normal adult encounter group, where new relationships are facilitated in a loose manner. But it did offer the opportunity to meet people within the boundaries of a religiously structured weekend.

Our first lunch together was after praying all Saturday morning and discussing the Torah, which was very stimulating. Here I was, looking around to see which, if any, women there were physically appealing and who could light a spark of initial interest within me. People were seated at tables of approximately 10 each. At lunch, the rabbis asked, "What have you gotten out of the *Shabbaton* so far and what new *mitzvah* or G-dly command would you like to take on and incorporate into your life?"

I listened to the responses each person gave. Based on the responses, the list I'd mentally made with three women on it winnowed down to one. The intellectual aspect of a relationship is just as important to me as the physical.

Focus is good. I set a goal to try to meet and to get to know a little better, one woman who might, G-d willing, be a suitable partner in my quest to establish a new, blended family.

That evening, a comic performed for the group. It was dark in the room, which gave me more confidence to move next to the woman I was attracted to and begin a conversation.

"Do you mind if I sit here?" I asked.

Her lukewarm response was not overwhelming. But then again, she didn't ask me to leave either.

We chatted, nothing profound as there was a performance going on, but I felt we bonded a little.

The next morning, the scheduled activity was to travel by bus in different groups to the *Ohel*, the grave site of the past *Rebbe*, or leader of the entire *Chabad* movement. In Chassidic cultures (of which there are many) each has a leader or *Rebbe*. *Chabad* has a history of seven Rebbes, going back to the late 1700s. The most recent one passed away in 1993 and had not been replaced. Despite no replacement, the movement had grown in quantum leaps since his passing. This was a testament to his belief that he wanted to create leaders, not followers, combined with another belief that a *tzaddik*, or holy man, lives on in his influence in even greater ways than during his physical life because his soul is no longer constrained by his body. The *Ohel* is considered a very holy place. People of all persuasions and levels of observance flock to the Ohel in order to petition the *Rebbe* for blessing of health, wealth and family.

So this was an auspicious location to meet my prospective partner. I was coming out of the *Ohel* just as she was getting off the bus. Flushed with the confidence and holy feeling engendered by my time in the *Ohel*, Marcela—the woman destined to become my wife, partner and mother of our children—and I connected in a very strong manner that day on the sidewalk.

We agreed to talk later as I was leaving and she was heading into the *Ohel*. Later was a goodbye gathering for the *Shabbaton* participants where the keynote speaker was giving a lecture on meditation.

Within 45 minutes I asked nearly 100 questions about her, her life, her goals and anything else I could think about asking. By the time we both had to leave we had exchanged business cards and promised to get in touch soon. She was shocked that I was leaving so quickly—without an opportunity to go out for coffee or dinner—but I had a plane to catch. We reluctantly said goodbye.

A week later, I had the urge to write her a heartfelt letter. This was before the days of the internet and email—for me, at least. She received my letter and wrote one in response, inviting me to visit her and her family in Argentina. This was December 1995, in the midst of winter. It didn't take long to recognize that a beautiful woman who I wanted to get to know better wanted me to visit her in a warm climate. As they say, my bags were already packed.

The rest is history. Two years of back-and-forth travel combined with a growing love for each other and a realization that we had mutual goals and a commitment to accomplish them. We married in December 1997 and today have a blended family of nine children and five grandchildren.

Thirteen-years ago, our youngest child, Chaya Sara was bornn. She was born with Down syndrome, and I remember distinctly the surgeon coming to ask me what I thought were strange questions right after her birth. It reached the point where I asked him why he was questioning me this way.

He replied, "There is a 98 percent chance she has Down syndrome."

"What do you mean 98 percent?" I asked.

The doctor was certain she did, as there were very obvious physical characteristics she displayed, such as splayed feet. I huddled with my wife to share this news, and said, "If this is what G-d has willed, it must be for the best, and we should consider ourselves fortunate."

This was the biggest understatement of my life.

Chaya is an extraordinary source of love to all and is the glue for our family. With her older siblings, she has had the benefit of a lot of good role modeling, love and probably has matured in her street smarts way beyond what you might anticipate. Seven years ago she was diagnosed with AML, child leukemia. It was a shock to our collective system. Fortunately, with her strong will and indomitable attitude, as well as the excellent medical care we received at University Hospitals Health System, today she is cancer free and thriving.

We are all so grateful for being blessed with such a child and the love she brings to everyone she comes in contact with. In fact, she embodies the idea of adding meaning to life.

Today, I recognize that meeting Marcela was a turning point in my life. I had accomplished the beginning of my dream for rich family life, grounded in G-dly ideals and connection. That is what I would call keeping my feet on the ground and my head in the sky.

### *Principle*

Add meaning to life by having faith
and striving for higher aspirations
while remaining grounded.

# Chapter 6

*"The greatest gift I can give you is the ability
to learn how to stand on your own two feet."*

In 1970, I graduated from The Ohio State University.
My goal had always been to become an attorney,
so I began taking steps for the next phase of my
education—law school.

Howard Metzenbaum, an attorney who went
on to have a successful business career before
becoming a U.S. Senator, was a close friend of my
dad's. I was fortunate to get a job filing papers and
doing errands at Howard's law offices when I was a
teenager. I loved the hustle, bustle and professional
air of the partners and his firm. Howard's success
in the business world—becoming a partner in
APCOA (Airport Parking Company of America)—
demonstrated that the legal profession offered
numerous opportunities for people beyond
just practicing law. I also saw one of my cousins,
Donald Kottler, move to California and become
an extremely successful personal injury attorney.
These were excellent role models for me to follow.

Smitten with being an attorney, I applied and was accepted to Cleveland-Marshall College of Law.

There was one problem with my plans: Although the law school was reasonably priced—especially compared to today's costs—my father reiterated the fact that while he wanted to provide me with an undergraduate degree, my graduation from Ohio State signaled my financial independence. Thus, the burden of paying for law school fell on my shoulders.

The solution seemed simple: Get a job, and work during the day while going to law school at night. I asked my father if I could come work for the family business. He reluctantly agreed, and so my career began in the one business I never thought I would have much to do with.

Training was largely nonexistent. It initially consisted of hitting the road with a younger salesperson my dad had hired and applying tips I picked up from my Uncle Abe. Fortunately, the business grew as I grew to love the business. And, while I loved my dad, I did not love his role as my taskmaster. Compliments were few and far between, and the most maddening thing was his endless desire to discuss the business, at all times of day, in all places, so I felt like I never had a respite from it. Things finally came to a head five years later when I was diligently studying for the bar exam.

As I was studying, my father would call: "Can't you charge two cents more for the oleo on this order, David?" my father would ask. "The market is up."

"Dad, I'm studying."

"Well," he said, "I'm looking at the order and think we can make a few more bucks here."

Finally, I put my foot down.

"Dad, I understand, but passing the bar exam on the first try is very important to me. I need time to study and not think about the business."

Reluctantly, my father gave me the space I needed. Learning to be independent led to my later ability to become self-sufficient. I had to separate myself from the business and my dad so that I could pursue my own interests and be successful. At times, I had to keep my own counsel as well. Despite his constant barrage of advice, questions and comments, Dad actually often told me to think selfishly. "Do what you think is best for you," he said. I'm sure all of his mentoring—and hectoring—was, in my dad's mind, in my best interest because "the greatest gift he could give me was the ability to learn how to stand on my own two feet."

The situation created a somewhat stressful relationship with my father. I knew he loved me very much and wanted me to be successful, but at times I was resentful that he was so much tougher on me than on my younger siblings. I also felt that at times there was even a little bit of jealousy in my dad—perhaps shades of those old Greek tragedies. In any event, as Jewish Law tells us, giving another the chance to be self-sufficient is the highest form of giving.

It is critically important for parents and mentors to try to instill this lesson of self-sufficiency into their charges. Few things are better than knowing you're prepared for whatever contingencies life may throw at you, as well as being confident you're able to take accountability for your actions, look at life realistically, and admit your mistakes so that you can learn and move on. We live in a very connected world, and although one of our basic instincts is to connect with others, knowing you can survive and thrive on your own is critical to being successful in life and business.

Having confidence in yourself also provides a stronger foundation for building relationships with others, which is one of the most satisfying aspects of my business and professional career. "No man is an island unto himself" isn't just a saying, it's a fact. One of the best lessons I've learned is how to establish win-win relationships and to add value to every relationship I'm involved with. That's important because when you are self-sufficient—

and confident—you look for ways to add value rather than simply extract it.

Keep in mind, however, that not everyone is a potential relationship. You want to find others who share your values and ideals. Look below the surface in order to better understand others' intentions and, as my father said, give the benefit of the doubt while remembering that trust is sacred and once broken is nearly impossible to regain. Like many things in life, this is a balancing act. What you see is not always black and white, but rather shades of gray. This is especially true when wanting to make a contribution to others—adding meaning to someone's life. In Rath's "Fully Charged," he discusses how we need to look at ways to add daily happiness in our lives and talks about the little things we do to facilitate that. Rath breaks this down into three basic categories:

- Daily interactions.
- Energy created by our eating, moving and sleeping.
- Adding meaning to our lives.

He defines "meaning" as the things we do for others that are so much more satisfying than what we do for ourselves. This concept seems congruent with the idea that when we learn to stand on our own two feet we have the security and willingness to make a contribution whenever and however we can.

After my father and I grew the business—with both top- and bottom-line revenue—it was my pleasure to find ways to pay him back for the opportunity he'd given me and the mentoring he provided. I loved being able to take him and the family out for frequent meals and pay for them. It made me feel more like a man, having grown up and taken responsibility for the bill. Our successes also prompted me to ask my father to keep increasing his salary—it was only appropriate because he allowed me to keep increasing mine.

Despite this, things were not always so rosy. There were difficult lessons we learned along the way, as well as serious differences of opinion between my father and I in our approaches to growing the company and physically accommodating the growth. Dad loved delving into things, absorbing all the details and taking his time coming to a decision. This was reflected in the way he enjoyed his meals as well—with a deliberate, time-consuming approach. He often chastised me for moving too fast, whether it was eating or making decisions.

I disagreed with him on this point. My approach was more intuitive, I argued. I trusted my gut instincts, which served me well. Sure, I was a little impatient with what seemed the trivial details, but once we had the concept determined those things needed less attention. And perhaps I was also less of a perfectionist than my father, willing to adapt as things happened and circumstances changed.

One example of our conflicts occurred during the planning phase of our expanded building project. We had outgrown our physical space and luckily, we had excess land adjacent to our current building which could accommodate a 20,000-square-foot expansion. Although I was advised by our general contractor and architect that it could be less expensive to build elsewhere because the subsurface of our property was an old landfill, which would require extra cost to support the larger building and product loads, this thought was anathema to me. It would mean I was abandoning the property my dad had picked, and that just wouldn't do. We moved ahead with the planning process.

There were a few hiccups in the early stages of the project, but we hired a good architect and an excellent general contractor. The process of working on the project drove me bananas. I must have authorized literally dozens of plans for the layout of the offices and warehouse. The office layout, itself, was a fascinating puzzle. My father, being the perfectionist he was, tried to anticipate every potential traffic flow and all the internal movement of our team. He would approve one plan, then think more about it and return with new modifications. It was mind-numbing. From my perspective, we needed to move and get the project started. I tried to see things from my dad's point of view, but oftentimes wanted to repeat his litany of sayings back to him during our regular times of conflict.

Finally, I said, "Dad, we can't prepare for every contingency. I think we have done the best we can here to think about and plan for them, but we need to move ahead or we will lose the bank financing we have in place."

The potential of losing our working capital lit a spark underneath him. He signed off on the final plans and we were able to move forward.

But that was just one conflict; we had many. For years, we had an asphalt driveway that got progressively worse and eventually stood in a state of terrible disrepair. There were chuckholes big enough to break a car axle, which was problematic because people would work their way from the street to our building to take advantage of the "open to the public" opportunity to buy institutional-type food products not generally available to the public at "wholesale prices." I put that in quotes as our pricing was between what we sold at wholesale and what retailers charged for the products. It was a winning formula as that line of our business grew to be $1 million on its own.

To my point, I was concerned that we did not have a proper driveway—not just for the public but to handle the increased truck traffic carrying loads of food in and out. After some research, I found one of the major disadvantages of asphalt was that it is very susceptible to water damage. If water was not properly running off the property it would erode whatever new driveway we put in. My philosophy was build it once—correctly—and not find ourselves in a constant state of damage and repairs. The cost to do it right? $75,000—a lot of money in 1980. My father once again reluctantly signed off.

The job entailed the contractor literally ripping up the existing driveway and re-sculpturing the land to accommodate the proper water runoff. We were located in a low area, close to the flood zone, so it made things challenging.

One day, in the middle of the process, I was pulling into work when my father came flying out of the office screaming, "What did I think I was doing, ruining the driveway?"

This was not the first or last time he would second-guess the project—and me with it. I seriously contemplated packing my bags and leaving. It was likely the deep-seated feeling of wanting to honor my father, alongside with the practical considerations of walking away from everything I had helped build that kept me there. As I mentioned, things were not always so rosy in our business relationship—but we persevered together. We all have internal conflicts with our good side—full of values and spiritual aspirations—and our animal side—full of longing for selfish pleasures.

My own struggle with my father revolved around a number of key issues. First, there was the desire to earn my independence and self-sufficiency, which contrasted with his own ideas of what was best for me or the business. Next, there was my need to be loyal, grateful, and to honor him and his contributions, which was at odds with my strong distaste for some of his business practices and general attitude that he always had a lesson to teach me. Both were inflamed by what I always saw as his preference for my siblings as I felt he wasn't as tough on them as he was on me.

In retrospect, I have come to realize that perhaps the more one cares about something the more effort he or she puts into it. So in some ways, perhaps Dad was just telling me he loved me—but in his own way. I know he loved all of his children deeply. He was a wonderful father in that regard. And he often made the humorous comment, "I would not take a $1 million for any of them, but I would not give you a penny for another one."

Every experience—good and bad—was filed away in my memory. In fact, that led to the great epiphany I had when my father told the nurse on his deathbed, "Tell David I love him."

While we had tremendous conflict, I so greatly appreciated the lessons he imparted and the strength that was forged through our conflict and working together. Ultimately, the experiences enabled me to learn how to stand on my own two feet—and isn't that in itself a valuable lesson?

### Principle

Learn not to depend on others
and to be self-sufficient.

# Chapter 7

*"Business should be fun."*

*"Have a sense of humor."*

*"Profit is not a dirty word."*

*"Volume is secondary to profit."*

Nothing made my father happier than when he made a smart purchase or outwitted the competition and made a "good buck." He loved to tell the story about how one day there was a shortage of tomatoes and he opportunistically found a vendor with a truckload. He promptly purchased all the tomatoes, took them to a neighborhood where there was a shortage, and made a killing. I remember a similar story he told about a natural disaster in New York, which occurred when he was visiting as a teenager. As he told it, the boardwalk had no food. He was able to find some he could sell, then hustled over to the boardwalk and sold out of everything in minutes.

My father always said that business should be fun, and you should have a sense of humor about things.

Those are very lofty and difficult goals—especially when things are not going well or according to plan. It's one of those sayings that sounds good in principle, but can be elusive in practice. As I observed my father for many years in his work habitat—and as a child in my formative years—it never seemed liked he was having much fun in the business. Dad did have an innate sense of humor that kept him going. He also had a keen sense of value, timing and retentive ability, which enabled him to persevere. It's one of the reasons he ended up as the sole owner of the business after years of strife among family members. Nevertheless, this caused problems within the family dynamic of the business, but that's a story for another day.

Unfortunately, in most of my business experience—as well as my father's—serendipitous profit stories were few and far between. So it's no wonder that it's taken me a long time to incorporate the principle of having fun and being profitable into my life. Due to my father's continuous reminders, the seeds of this great idea were sown within me at an early age.

Having fun is important. We spend so much of our time at work. If we are fortunate enough to be in business for ourselves as entrepreneurs, it provides the opportunity to make this time meaningful, and hopefully tie it to our mission. That's what gives us the passion and determination to persevere long enough that we're able to support ourselves and our family, and, if done correctly, be able to give something back to our communities and favorite causes.

We are well aware business has its ups and downs. I was fortunate in the first eight years of my career to enjoy tremendous growth and profitability in our business. I really liked getting to know people and communicating with them. I enjoyed being able to strike up friendships, to make new acquaintances, and to turn them into good customers. It was fun. I also loved developing new ideas and products so the people I was serving appreciated my dedication to going above and beyond for them. These traits motivated and propelled me to add new and innovative products to our existing products list, and pushed me to constantly seek items that would be more valuable than commodity-type items. While my father preferred to stay back at the ranch to focus on the logistics of running the company, I had the good fortune to focus on these areas to build the business.

Not until many years later—after I had lost the food distribution business and acquired an excellent business coach—was I able to recognize what made the start of my business career so fun and profitable: the 80/20 rule.

The 80/20 rule says that 20 percent of your clients, products or services can provide 80 percent of your profit. This rule can be extended even further to embrace the concept that there is also an 80/20 rule within the 80/20 itself. Under this definition, literally 4 percent of your activity, clients and resources produce 64 percent of your revenues. This can be a fun exercise if you're able to put it into practice.

A corollary concept goes along with this: If you focus on your strengths and natural abilities—versus trying to eliminate your weaknesses or to improve them—you will be much further ahead in reaching your goals. Of course, there are nuances, as well as alternate solutions, like hiring people to be strong in areas where you are weak. But when I was in my late 20s and early 30s, I did not comprehend all of this.

In retrospect, I realize that when you are struggling to stay afloat, deal with the bank, vendors, customers, employees, and in my case, my father and uncle, it's easy to see how work stopped being fun. It became more necessary to work in the office instead of on the road. This came about because of growth and poor health.

First, our company was in the midst of natural growth and evolution, going from 15 employees to 50. About the same time, we opened a new,

30,000-square-foot warehouse on the site where we used to operate out of 10,000 square feet.

Then came the first of several serious health incidents involving my father. He had a mini stroke, which thankfully did not impair him mentally but necessitated him being in a hospital for a period of time. He was admonished by his doctors that he needed to take it easier in the future.

Most business owners would agree that growing a business—building revenue, adding new products, and expanding the number of employees— can become somewhat overwhelming for a young entrepreneur with no previous business management experience and without a layer of middle management to help. Add to this the lack of an outside board and you're left with some lonely times where you're flying by the seat of your pants, which is not always so comfortable.

Into the office I came. My freedom on the road, as well as my ability to focus on my strengths and fun activities, became mired down in logistics, dealing with employee grievances, operations and the never-ending quest to cut expenses. These were all necessary areas to focus on, but they most definitely were not fun. And as we continued to grow by leaps and bounds, adding more people, sales and products, the adage "volume is secondary to profit" became more and more apparent. We were not focused on our core group of products that were exclusive, like Häagen-Dazs, instead we began to sprout tendrils that snaked out in several different directions.

I analyzed the company and determined that because we had an entrée into Chinese restaurants, it seemed attractive to hire more sales people who were Asian to help service that part of the business. It was progress of a sort, but in the long run did not really benefit the business.

Eventually, our competitors caught up to us. Our secret products, which produced so much revenue for the company, were discovered by competitors as the restaurants starting asking them for similar products. As a result, our profit margins were squeezed. The same thing happened during our efforts to broaden our product range to more restaurants. This was a bad combination: increasing costs and lower margins. And it drew focus from our ice cream business. About the same time, we acquired the exclusive distribution rights for Dove Bars, Good Humor ice cream, and Ben and Jerry's. We ultimately lost exclusive distribution rights for Häagen-Dazs due to our refusal to drop Dove Bars—after they changed their mind about allowing us to carry the line and suddenly insisted we stop distributing it.

As a result, top-line revenue growth became our cover-up story for dwindling profit margins. The day of reckoning finally arrived when we realized we could not profitably support all the business we were doing and the bank demanded we improve our profits if we wanted to continue being lent money.

This wake-up call led us to restructure the company. Fortunately, we were to be able to settle with our food-service vendors, sell that portion of the business to a competitor, and move forward with a $4 million business that consisted solely of our exclusive lines and higher-profit products. We also streamlined our employee base from 100 people down to 35. With all this in place, we refocused the company on what was fun and profitable.

For a few years this formula worked well. But then the volume bug hit me again, and I decided we should become more of a major player in the ice cream distribution business. My first decision was to begin selling a more mainstream volume item, and settled on a half-gallon line.

To say I was stupid would be an understatement. This type of product was the commodity item I'd shied away from my entire business life, but suddenly the numbers seemed workable. What I failed to realize at the time was that the sheer cost of storing, distributing and sharing in marketing expenses—

for the first time on a product—far exceeded the gross profit we made on each case of ice cream. As a result, after 18 months of successful market penetration, we sold 1 million cases, and lost $1 on every case. It was an unmitigated disaster!

I should have listened to the stories my father told me about my Grandma Esther's philosophy—she wanted to only make 1 percent, which in her mind meant buying a product for a buck and selling it for $2, which showed her good instincts. Instead, I ended up losing a business that today is valued at more than $10 million and represents more than 40 percent of all the ice cream sold in Northeast Ohio. Talk about a hard lesson to learn! This was certainly a costly and painful one.

The warning signs were there. Certainly, had I spent the time to take a closer look at the numbers and to analyze not just the percentage of profit to be derived but also the hidden costs, the problems could have been avoided. As any business person who has navigated his or her way through the ups and downs of business knows, good advice is sometimes hard to come by, and the questions we should be forced to ask can be the most valuable advice we can get.

After the collapse, I was forced to reflect on the many successes I had in the food business as well as the very difficult times and challenges I experienced.

This was even more challenging because my father was not available due to his increasing health problems. I had counted on him as my rock in times of trouble, and he had served as a great source of emotional support and comfort. But as my father became frailer and had a continuing series of incidents that necessitated major operations, the thought of his worsening condition disturbed me. Perhaps, however, it also gave me some sense of freedom—recognizing on some subconscious level that he was no longer there, I was ready to move on—hopefully to pastures that were more fun.

At no other time in my life was my dad's adage, "Good judgment comes from experience; unfortunately, experience comes through bad judgment" so startlingly clear.

### *Principle*

Be engaged and focused, and your business will become fun.

# Chapter 8

*"There is more than one way to get downtown."*

From the time I was very young, my natural instinct was to forge my own path. Perhaps the fact that I got a mild case of polio at the age of 6 reinforced these instincts because I was forced to spend several months in a hospital. It was a scary experience. However, one of the side benefits— beyond the love I felt whenever my parents would come to visit me—was the opportunity to become an avid and excellent reader. To say I had a lot of time on my hands is an understatement, but I loved to learn and to take adventures in the pages of the books I read. It's something that has remained with me today, and I still read at least two books every week. I'm sure this love of learning—and ability to imagine—aided my creativity and communication skills.

My instinctive yearning to learn, combined with an inquisitive personality, led me to embrace the idea of finding more than one way to get things accomplished. It didn't hurt that I was somewhat of a rebel as well.

This doesn't mean I was finding and taking shortcuts. In fact, my dad always impressed me with the notion that "the shortest distance between two points was a straight line." Instead, it meant being willing to strike out on my own with something new if the current path did not seem attractive. Maybe it's because I'm ambidextrous—I write and eat left-handed and play sports right-handed—but whatever the reason, this idea simply resonated with me.

When I started my official career in my father's food distribution business, there was no formal training. "Training" consisted of being told to "go out and sell something," and being instructed to work with two of the company's outside sales reps to get some real-life experience. One of those reps was my dear Uncle Abe; the other was a young man with a sense of humor.

Abe was one of those very colorful characters that could charm the birds out of the trees but could also land you—and him—in some real predicaments. What he lacked in sound judgment he more than made up for with optimism, grit and a loving personality. Unfortunately, his love for my father was not evident. The brothers would fight like cats and dogs. It only took a sideways look or wrong word to launch a screaming match.

These seemingly never-ending skirmishes took place in our small office space of approximately 800 square feet, where everyone had an opportunity for a ringside seat. Making matters worse, my dad had established an innovative direct-to-consumer, cash-and-carry business, which meant customers came in to the same space. Just like Old Faithful could be expected to explode each day, my father and uncle could be counted on to explode each day— more often than not in front of poor, unsuspecting customers who just entered the offices to pick up some frozen food or delicacies at wholesale prices. Little did they know that drama and entertainment were included in the package.

Like many families in business, although my father and uncle loved each other, money and business have a nasty way of creating problems. My uncle always harbored resentment that my dad obtained his share of the business for less than what it was worth. Of course, my uncle was precluded from earning any big income as he had a bad habit of neglecting to report to and pay Uncle Sam. So Abe got even by not giving much effort for the business.

All of this dramatically changed when I started achieving some real sales success and Uncle Abe, who was extremely determined, decided he would show me who could really sell. This transformation became a tremendous benefit for the company because as I started branching out in handling seafood and frozen shellfish, Abe developed an amazing rapport and success in selling ultimately all of the Chinese restaurants within a 100-mile radius. Soon our annual seafood sales climbed to more than $4 million, which reflected a 10-fold increase in our overall business revenue from when I first started full time with the company.

As our business flourished, there were plenty of opportunities for innovation and calculated risk purchasing. I knew from my first days on the road that I hated being asked, "What is the price today?" on the items that were really commodities. Early on I started looking for "blind items," as my dad called them. Blind items were more unique than the traditional commoditized products, commanded a premium price, and added value to the company. One of these blind items was small shrimp, which was used for egg rolls and many other dishes the Chinese restaurants served instead of paying for— and cutting up—bigger shrimp. I always had an eye for good products and the benefits of establishing excellent rapport with my suppliers through loyalty and fair dealings. This "smaller shrimp" idea for our Chinese restaurant customers was one such example. Important also was the concept of trying to locate one main supplier, so that I could purchase all of their available product in my area. This helped enhance our company's brand awareness as the supplier-of-choice for that specific product. It was my good fortune that I met such a supplier at one of the conventions I went to and we developed a very fruitful relationship that lasted for years.

The "Elephant" brand became famous in our area and developed into the brand of choice for many local restaurants because they liked its consistency and sweet flavor, as well as the favorable pricing. We bought them sized at 50/60 per pound all the way to 200/300 per pound. The most attractive thing for me was that we discovered this opportunity before our competitors did, so we were able to set the market price—and did so fairly. That allowed us to make a dollar-per-pound profit on a much lower cost product than the larger size shrimp, which sold for several dollars more but only provided profits between a quarter and 75 cents per pound.

This is one of the keys to being innovative in business. When selling a product or a service it really pays to identify the different components of the process or the value-added part of the products you offer. It also pays to find products that offer specific, unique benefits that match a client's needs.

Finally, timing can be critically important. In our case, we were the first to market and were able to set the price. But timing comes into play in other areas. For example, when you're dealing with products where the price fluctuates, you should try to buy ahead when the prices seem attractive. My father would say, "You're only as good as your buy," which meant that if you wanted to make money, you had to buy at the right time. This translated for me to stepping in and buying sometimes very large quantities of products when the price was good and we had an opportunity to maximize our profits. We had ample storage space and access to additional space we could rent, so it made sense to buy ahead whenever possible. I would do this with products ranging from rice and soybean oil to shortening, spareribs and all types of seafood that fit with our Chinese business.

One year there was a tremendous glut of shrimp on the market at harvest time. Suppliers were scrambling because they needed to freeze and move the product. They were running out of room and being pressured by their lenders to keep their product moving. This created a perfect storm for them and perfect opportunity for us to buy ahead and stock a full year's supply—more than 500,000 pounds, which I doled out at market condition prices as the year went on. Luckily for us, the prices nearly doubled within 60 days of our purchase. As Frank Sinatra so eloquently said: "That was a very good year."

But as I've mentioned, the food distribution business didn't last due to some serious errors in judgment. And so, after 23 years—some of them very rewarding; some of them very difficult—I was forced to strike out in a new career. The only thing I knew at the time was that I wanted to incorporate as many of the lessons and successes I achieved in the distribution business to my new financial planning career—and to keep the mistakes I'd made at a minimum. My gut instinct said I wanted to try to duplicate the niche position I had enjoyed for so many years with so many good products. How to duplicate that in a different field and to avoid being seen as providing a commodity product or service was the challenge. One big issue with the services industry is that most prospective clients want to label you quickly so they can dismiss the idea of needing to listen to what you have to say. That leads to the common refrain of, "My attorney handles everything" or "My CPA has me well set" or "I'm happy with my advisers." All of which makes the dreaded cold phone call trying to get quality appointments with people of wealth who might actually listen with an open mind an exercise in futility.

I also knew I did not want to employ any people— at least in the beginning—because I found that aspect of running a business the most difficult. At its peak, our food distribution business employed 100 people. That was big enough to give me plenty of headaches yet not big enough to have well-developed levels or layers of highly competent management. It is difficult to be a good sounding board for your employees and boss without getting dragged into a lot of interpersonal relationship issues with your employees. I wanted to have enough creative energy and focus to profitably grow the new business, so for me, that meant no startup employees.

I was intrigued by the products I was selling. Life insurance was very appealing because of the financial benefits it provides families, its potential to solve family and tax issues, its ability to generate large pay days, and its usefulness in conjunction with charitable planning, which was my true mission. I had no interest in handling investments, as I knew I could not be all things to all people, which was another one of my father's favorite sayings. For me, focus was paramount. By focusing on life insurance, specifically creating a way to avoid it being seen as a commodity sale, I was able to build a niche: incorporating the life insurance sale with a sophisticated planning process that utilized my legal background, professional contacts and outside-the-box thinking.

This was, of course, easier said than done. I achieved some early successes by acquiring a few clients of great wealth. But I struggled to learn as I went along, despite being recognized as the most successful "rookie agent" in Cuyahoga County for my first three years. Those areas where I was not successful bothered me. First, I wasn't able to spend as much time focused on increasing philanthropy through my work. Second, my business model required me to start each year with zero recurring revenue because I was not involved in investments and life insurance was not a product that paid much in the way of renewals. Finally, the case planning aspect could be very time consuming, and most of the time did not even result in a life insurance sale. Worse, getting qualified referrals to potential clients was a hit-and-miss proposition for a variety of reasons, not the least of which was the credibility factor of a friend or peer versus a referral from a professional servicing the client. As I tried to overcome these challenges I realized it was no wonder more than two-thirds of the people who entered the life insurance industry didn't stay with it.

I began to wonder where the Häagen-Dazs of insurance or planning was that I could ride exclusively on my horse to success. Did such a product exist or was it just a figment of my active and yearning imagination? I looked for ways to leverage my previous Häagen-Dazs magic to achieve a steady stream of qualified referrals from professionals whose referrals meant something. Someone once told me it would take 10 to 15 years to really understand any new business segment and be able to fully utilize that understanding to achieve a successful career. I scoffed at this notion because I thought I could parlay previous successes into being a quicker study. Thankfully, because I kept my eyes and ears open to new ideas, new contacts and innovative ways of doing things, I started to develop a repertoire of ideas, products and strategies I believed could be deployed for my clients' benefit.

These led to a moderate level of success, including some very high income years, but never generated the steady referrals I so desperately wanted. I was still searching for that better solution to match my persona—an established expert rather than just an idea person looking for a problem to solve. I wanted something that allowed me to be much more focused, and to be recognized as someone they should refer clients to, because I was able to incorporate many good ideas. To me, this setup would yield more attorneys and CPAs who wanted to turn over their most valuable clients to me. It wasn't until I hired a business coach who helped me peel away the veneer and see the business within my business that my career really started to take off.

My business coach worked with me to explore what had brought me the most success over the past 24 months. Together, we discovered it was in the review process of client's insurance portfolios. That process enabled me to bring the most value-added services to clients because it employed my creative nature. That, of course, translated into higher revenues and more referrals from those all-important centers of influence because their clients were very happy with the work I was doing for them. It also led to additional revenues for the referral source and me to share, which of course we did with full transparency to the client. Finally, I was not perceived as selling something but rather providing a valuable service—a service that over a recent 12-month period delivered more than $15 million in cash and tax benefits to my clients.

Looking back, when I was in the distribution business I was always most effective when I was operating on both the buy and sell side of an equation. This gave me a keener awareness of true market conditions and enabled me to stay one step ahead of others on the knowledge curve.

The Holy Grail, if you will, occurred when I discovered that life settlements—the business of helping life policy owners sell their policies to a third-party market buyer rather than let it lapse or surrender to the issuing carrier for minimum value—could be a key strategy to helping clients with existing polices. The average amount of extra revenue a client obtains from his policy (if it prices well in the market) is 800 percent of what he or she would receive on surrender. When you think about it, that's pretty amazing.

I started poking around, asking why so few agents took advantage of this process and learned that some carriers wouldn't let their agents do so, some broker-dealers prohibited it, and others were just lazy and didn't want to learn new strategies. But what this process does is put the client in the driver's seat. It aligns the interest of the client and the agent—in this case, me—because I receive a percentage of the net value I add to the equation. The more value, the more I receive and the more the client receives—this is a true win-win solution. Think of it like a tax reduction specialist CPA who also does all the upfront work and in return receives a percentage of the savings he or she creates. This is only one component of the Million Dollar Life Insurance Rescue™ process, albeit a very effective one.

Sometimes competitors say that I essentially do life insurance reviews, but that's downplaying the importance of the exercise. It's akin to saying that the chefs in the best restaurants are just "cooking" like the cooks in local greasy spoons. The reality is that there is a very big difference in the output and outcomes.

I look at things from a legal and tax perspective to ascertain whether clients may be at risk for myriad potential issues. Perhaps the client, for example, has been advised that he can stop paying premiums and borrow them from his cash values. That sounds good unless the policy lapses before the client's death, in which case there will be a large phantom income tax levied by the IRS for forgiveness of debt. I have seen dozens of instances like these, so a loan rescue strategy has evolved to handle the variety of situations that can arise through this particular piece of bad advice.

It's hard to believe, but more than 69 percent of policies today have no agent associated with them, which means no one is servicing the policy. These so-called "orphan polices" demonstrate the serious need clients have for assistance in having their insurance reviewed frequently. Add to this the issue that many agents simply do not have time or are not compensated for keeping up regular reviews of the polices they have sold, and you begin to see the scope of the problem for policy owners. This is why the insurance carriers' dirty little secret is that

90 percent of all the life policies written will never get paid at maturity (the client's death) because they lapse before maturity. This issue screams "service problem," and it's an area I realized my unique skill set was perfect to tackle. And so, I found myself once again living one of my father's sayings by figuring out what "downtown" was and working backward to create a path forward.

### *Principle*

Creativity and innovation lead to success. When you think outside the box, you look for unique nontraditional solutions.

# Chapter 9

*"Always look at things from the other person's viewpoint."*

*"Whose ax is being ground?"*

Outings with my father, unfortunately, were rare growing up. We went to dinner together—especially after I moved in with him after my parents divorced and my mother remarried. Fun outings though were scarce. There was an occasional Browns game with my brother, dad and me, but not too often.

I had just turned 16 when my mother remarried. She and my dad had gone through a difficult and protracted divorce that took three long years. I became accustomed to being the man of the house. So it should come as no surprise that I was very uncomfortable when her new husband moved into our house and wanted to impose rules and restrictions on us children.

I'm sure his intentions were good. As this was his first marriage, my mother's new husband had no experience as a father and his disciplinary tactics were not welcomed. I missed my dad's warmth, as well as his acceptance of me as I was. The end result was that I moved out of the house one month later, leaving my mother and siblings behind. It was a very difficult time in my life. Luckily, my father took me in.

I learned a lot about my father during this time. For example, when a new bowling alley was built a few miles from our home it included a beautiful billiards room. I was delighted—and quite frankly surprised—to discover my father liked to play pool. He lined up combination shots and sank the balls very easily, which was astounding to me at the time. Looking back, I think this reflected his innate understanding of how things worked together, and his ability to think a few steps ahead.

Perhaps it was a sense of physical perspective that guided Dad's grasp of the billiards table, but more likely it was simply part of his overall ability to see things in a larger context. He dealt with people very well and was an excellent negotiator because he could figure out where they were coming from in their perspective of the deal.

To be honest, many of Dad's deals weren't designed to be long-lasting; but some were, and grew into longtime friendships and even stronger business relationships. It was following his lead in this area that helped me hone my negotiating skills and become a strong negotiator myself. And it fits nicely into understanding that your ability to sell is based on your ability to buy right. As I developed my own approach, I acquired a sixth sense for the timing of deals, listening carefully to sellers' voices for hints of uncertainty or information I could use to know when to buy more and when to buy less.

The ability to negotiate a strong but fair deal helped me numerous times also in establishing long-term, favorable, exclusive types of relationships for distribution rights for many excellent products, including Häagen-Dazs, Dove Bars and Good Humor ice cream. Combining these type of business relationships with always taking advantage of "buy-in deals" and price discounts for prompt pay added up to literally millions of dollars in profits over the years. What this means is that learning to negotiate well is an art form that people in business pay good money to learn. Negotiation techniques come into play not just in business, of course, but in politics, environmental rights, labor disputes and just about every aspect in life.

When I lost my food business and had to start a new career in the financial services field, that ability and necessity to negotiate became critical. My experience negotiating prices and relationships in order to establish win-win scenarios would serve me well in the difficult profession of selling life insurance to wealthy clients. My original financial services manager warned me that there are always one or more obstacles standing in the way of closing deals in virtually every case.

First, there's competition. Second, professional adviser interference. And finally, bad underwriting of the actual insurance offer itself, in terms of the rate class to be used for the offer.

Each issue had to be negotiated. Sometimes it called for splitting a case with another adviser if there were some compelling reasons at play. Maybe they were the prospect's current agent and had a pre-existing relationship that needed to be addressed so that the prospect didn't have to choose between offers. Sometimes it was better not to split a case because the reasons given by the other agent were weaker, his relationship was weaker, or your case was more compelling on its own merits and it was a good idea to make the prospect choose. There was always a juggling act that included a lot of variables. Despite this, the firm principle I have always tried to adhere to is do whatever is in the best interests of the client. If his or her interests are always kept paramount, things always work out best in the long run. It is always much more fun—and better for everyone—when you are delivering solutions rather than selling something.

Underwriting is always a struggle. Choosing the best qualified personnel to represent you in that process is key. It makes negotiations easier and more productive. Timing is very important, as oftentimes better deals can be had at the end of the year when insurance carriers have a certain amount of business they want to put on the books and standards may be relaxed. It hasn't been an easy learning curve, but I have been delighted over the past eight years or so to effectively apply the buy/sell mechanics that worked best in the food business to the insurance business. This has made it easier to secure the best deal and offer it to clients. And it's the perspective of knowing the true value and negotiating for the best prices for the client that often comes to the forefront of my life these days when serving as a Life Insurance Doctor™ for my clients. Knowing when to buy and when to sell, and understanding what the real value is of the policies involved, has been invaluable in my ability to deliver the best results.

The settlement process over the past 20 years has become a very consumer friendly process. This process means that owners of life insurance can sell their policies to third-party buyers. Today, this is a $25 billion business. Previously, policy owners only had one choice if they did not want to keep their life insurance policy: surrender it to the issuing carrier for the cash surrender value net of any existing surrender charges. By having an open market to approach—and being able to create an auction process amongst buyers—it's now possible to garner an average of eight times as much money for the policy owners as they would receive on a surrender. This is truly an area where a lot of negotiating comes in. Fighting for the best deal for the clients is a lot of fun. It's profitable, too, as my fee is based on how successful I am for them.

In their book, "Friend & Foe," authors Adam Galinsky and Maurice Schweitzer lay out a compelling case for when to cooperate, when to compete, and how to succeed at both. The authors argue that what distinguishes man from all animals—other than the dolphin—is the ability to look in the mirror and realize he is looking at himself. This usually happens around the age of two. The other human characteristic they describe, which is equally powerful—and no other species on earth can duplicate—is the ability to see the world from another's perspective.

According to the authors, this test is measured by placing a child on one side of a model of three mountains that gradually increase in size from left to right. A doll is then placed on the other side. First, you ask the child to draw what the mountains look like from his or her perspective. Then, you ask the child to draw what the mountains look like from the doll's perspective. Most 4-year-olds get this task wrong—they will make both drawings look the same, from their perspective. Around age five, this changes. Children begin to realize the drawing should be flipped and are able to draw the mountains from the doll's perspective.

This ability to have a clear perspective is useful in nearly every aspect of our lives—from dealing with emergencies to engaging in business to handling family and marriage relationships. It reminded me of what my father used to say: "Try to see things from the other's point of view."

When you are engaged in negotiations and unaware of where the other person is coming from, the results can become costly. If you fail to understand what their needs are, or even the circumstances surrounding their behavior, you are much less likely to come away with a win-win scenario.

Not every deal can be consummated, of course, but when you approach negotiations with a clear understanding and respect for where each side is, you're able to achieve much better results. Having an open mind also opens up the possibility of dialogue and brainstorming, which further leads to equitable and mutually profitable results. My dad often said, "If two people have good will and an open mind when they sit down to talk, much more can be accomplished."

Despite not having a formal higher education or the advantage of the highly sophisticated methods they use today to measure human behavior, my dad's instincts were spot on: When you have perspective in negotiations, good things can—and will—happen.

## Principle

If you want to be a strong negotiator, you must understand— and appreciate—the importance of perspective.

# Chapter 10

*"I believe in human power."*

My father was a self-made man and independent thinker. His family had very little in the way of material possessions when he was a youngster, and as a result was exposed to the value of hard work when he was just 10 or 11 years old. My dad accompanied his father on visits to outlying farms where they purchased eggs and chickens, put them on the family's truck, then brought the goods back to sell out of Grandma's retail store, which was based in their house.

These early travails taught my father a lot about the world, including how to drive a truck long before he was of driving age. He learned about relationships, how to honor others, as well as fight discrimination and unfairness. These were values that stayed with him for the rest of his life. My grandfather had an African-American helper, who accompanied the two of them on his truck. Often they traveled to farms too far away for a return trip that day. When that happened, the farmer from whom my grandfather was buying goods would offer, "You and your son can stay in the house, but your helper has to sleep in the barn."

My grandfather and father would politely respond, "No thank you. If the barn is good enough for him, we'll stay there also."

It was through these stories of his youth that I gained an appreciation for my father's experiences and the wisdom he attained living them. His strong belief in the dignity of all people, regardless of their color, was something he passed to me early on. It came into play often, including when he introduced me to friends who were African-American. One such man, Mr. Oswald, was well-educated and a man of refinement. I remember the fondness and honor he bestowed upon my father during their interactions. Seeing the mutual respect between the two men left me with quite an impression.

Respecting others is one of the most important principles, and is the basis for all human interaction. It is the foundation for any successful relationship, and becomes the social lubricant that can create and sustain them, whether they are spousal, family, parental, business, or friendships. My father was very sensitive to perceived slights to his respect, and I remember on more than one occasion I got my behind hit with a belt (not the buckle) for being disrespectful.

One of the more humorous incidents I remember with fondness and alacrity was when my younger brother and I shared a bedroom next to our parents' bedroom. Noise carried in the house, and my father heard our late-night conversations.

He yelled out, "If I hear one more peep out of you, you'll be sorry."

My wise-ass nature usually got the best of me. "Peep, peep," I'd reply, often just to get a laugh out of my brother. While he might have found it funny, Dad didn't, and he come charging in telling me I needed to learn a lesson.

As he got ready to belt my behind, he said, "This is going to hurt me worse than it's going to hurt you."

"Of course," I responded, "why not save us both the pain then?"

Unfortunately, the beating was already in motion and my comments never earned me a reprieve.

Nevertheless, my father had great respect for all men, but saved a special respect for men of great intellect and values. He was not afforded the opportunity to go to college, despite being his high school's valedictorian, because his family did not have the funds to send him. However, Dad was a lifelong learner and took some college courses later in life. He often told me he drove his teachers crazy with so many questions in his attempts to get to the heart of what he was learning.

His thirst for knowledge was instilled in me, and I, in turn, had great respect for many of my teachers at Ohio State, and especially my law school professors. We had some brilliant professors at Cleveland-Marshall. Some were judges, some were practicing attorneys. One made a particularly profound impression on me. Hyman Cohen was my torts professor. I loved that class because it was so stimulating. I loved the mental process of determining relative liabilities or rights of plaintiffs and defendants, and the case law, which helped develop the formulas that would be used to determine those.

I'll never forget the case of proximate cause, with the underlying principal that we as humans need to be fully cognizant of the consequences of our actions, which are foreseeable. Issues like measuring the relative rights of individuals versus the rights of the social environment or society were fascinating in their complexity. We learned about how to deal with the rights of individuals who had been promised something and a promisor reneged on the deal. This type of case was specifically dealt with in our business law class, which dealt with the Uniform Commercial Code. This case law helped me pay for my entire legal education as I had reason to utilize it in one of my business dealings while I was going to law school.

Earlier, I mentioned that one of my techniques for growing the business was to try to be ahead of the curve and "buy right." One season, the shrimp prices were much lower than they had been in about 10 years. I decided to take the plunge and make a very large buy from a vendor I had not dealt with before. I wasn't sure he was dependable for either quality or reliable delivery, but the price was right and we made a deal that I would buy 10,000 pounds if the sample order of 2,500 pounds was good quality.

We received the first shipment, which was of acceptable quality. I requested the agreed upon remaining 7,500 pounds. Three weeks passed and I still hadn't received the remainder of the shipment, as promised, and wanted it delivered as soon as possible. The market was up $1.50 per pound and I was looking at a $10,000 profit—and an equal loss for the seller—based on the fluctuating price conditions.

Calls to the seller went unanswered. When I finally reached him by phone his excuse was that he had not yet shipped the remaining 7,500 pounds because he had not been paid for the first load. Even though the bill was not yet due, I replied, "I will come down to Alabama with a check for the first load and give it to you when I see my 7,500-pound balance being put on the commercial carrier who would deliver it to my warehouse."

The seller said, "Hmm…let me think about that." It was not exactly the answer I was seeking.

A few months went by without a word. I finally sent him a letter in which I explained that according to the U.C.C., I had the right to replace my shipment at current conditions and hold him accountable for the discrepancy in price for what I paid today and the price he had contracted for. At that point, I owed the supplier $10,000 for the partial shipment against the 50 cases that were delivered of the 200 promised. Since he never responded, I went out and bought the missing cases from another supplier at the current market prices. I was comfortable doing so because my net cost was the less expensive price I had been promised by the original seller. After I purchased the shrimp, I never paid the original supplier for the partial shipment. That $10,000 paid for my entire legal education.

This experience illustrated to me the principle that each of us has to follow through on our promises. To not do so is certainly a lack of respect and worse, immoral behavior.

When the time came for graduation from law school, my torts professor had become dean of the law school. He learned that although I planned to take the bar exam, I had no plans to practice law. He was a little upset and told me he believed I had a great facility and love for the legal-thinking process, but he understood my desire not to start over in a new profession when I was enjoying success and the thrill of building a business. I always fondly remembered our class and the discussions we had. My respect for the man, his talents and the perspective he imparted to me about the respect each person was due, both for their personal assets as well as their bodily assets, have stayed with me. Honesty is the best policy; following through on promises—these actions not only show respect for others but also allow us to respect ourselves.

Later in life, my father wrote a wonderful paper about human power. In it, he espoused the idea of inalienable rights of all humans—no matter what color—to receive dignity and respect. This strong ideal and value remains important to me. It's something that seems lacking in others. When you look at the world, the lack of respect for people, boundaries and property stand as a root cause for so much mayhem—from school children bullying their peers, to land grabs by Russia, to demonstrators fighting at political rallies. The common theme among all of these is an utter lack of respect for one's fellow man. It's one of those lessons that as I see what's unfolding around me I'm so grateful was driven into me at an early age. If more people had respect for others, many of the problems we face in the world may be much easier to solve.

## *Principle*

All men are created equal.
Treat people with dignity and
respect.

# *Chapter 11*

*"I'll do the best I can with no promises."*

*"I never want to break a promise."*

*"Once trust is broken, it's almost impossible to regain it."*

When someone provides more benefit to me than what is discussed, it greatly builds my respect for and trust in that person. Over my lifetime, I have relied on advice that was much more conservative than what the results actually were, which led to mutually beneficial gains.

When I was in the food business, I established a profitable relationship with one specific seafood producer who told me he would be able to deliver a certain amount of product and protect my exclusivity. This gentleman acted with integrity and consistently over-delivered his commitments. In return, he knew I could be counted on to regularly buy his product, be loyal and promptly pay my bills. This mutual trust led to a long, profitable relationship for both parties.

My father abhorred making promises. Because he would never commit to anything, it became one of the most frustrating aspects of growing up with him. Instead, he'd always say, "We'll see. I'll do the best I can." I never knew if it was because he did not want to commit or because he truly did not know if he would be able to fulfill the request.

As I reflect on this part of my life, I have come to realize that each of our early childhood experiences and the environment in which we grow up can greatly affect our views on life or our attitudes. Dad was a child of the Depression, so for him the uncertainty of his next meal or being used to living with very limited means was a pervasive influence on his attitudes and thinking.

I also came to realize that he was always there for me in a pinch—even without making that an overt promise. Growing up, we enjoyed a nice home, plenty of food and a good school to attend, but my dad was always hesitant to spend money on what he called luxuries. He explained there was a difference between necessities and luxuries, and I should get my head clear on the difference. Dad often teased me that, "I should be able to afford my own good tastes," saying I probably inherited those from my mother, who had grown up in a more affluent environment.

My father bought a piece of land adjacent to our food distribution center when he had to move from his prior location in the city after the government exercised its eminent domain rights. With his unerring instincts, he chose a very centrally located site—accessible to all areas before the roads to get there were even built. He was quite prescient. Dad used to refer to the extra land every time we bugged him about wanting to go on a family vacation, saying, "When I sell the land, we'll all go to the Concord, a fabulous resort in the Catskills."

When I was 18 years old, there was still no sale of Dad's land in sight. My senior year of high school was coming to an end and I prevailed upon my father to "take me to the Concord" alone, since my siblings, mother and her second husband were all living in a different city.

"OK," my father said, much to my surprise and delight.

And so, we piled into his Ford for a road trip.

When we arrived, the Concord was indeed a fabulous resort. The two of us shared a room. The food and entertainment were fantastic. And then, I discovered another form of entertainment that I loved at the time—gambling. The Concord had a poker room.

One night, I hurried down with a small stake I'd saved up. I played cards with a group of people at what could be deemed a moderate betting table. I got lucky and won about $400. With my confidence puffed up, I decided to try my hand at the bigger betting table, which of course had some real experts, or "sharpies," as my dad would say.

That game didn't go as well as the earlier one. When I had a flush, somebody had a full house. When I pulled a straight, someone played a flush. I was outclassed. Not only did I lose the $400 I had won, I ended up owing one of the other players an additional $500 for a bet I made on credit.

I was dismayed, to say the least.

Ironically, my mother was an excellent card player. So are my two sons, Jeremy and Zachary. Jeremy has actually become semi-famous on the professional poker tour, having been at three final tables and appeared on TV for his exploits. Zachary has been very successful at cards, too, although for him the game is just an avocation. He's much happier working full time as a commercial real estate broker. As for me, my luck and card-playing skills were not as developed as the three of them. I was down on my luck, in trouble and certainly not looking forward to the conversation I needed to have with my dad.

When I confronted him—with my tail between my legs—he wasn't too happy with my behavior. But he understood the jam I was in. It was important for him that I live up to my word, and my father gave me $500 to pay off my debt. I was chastised, but learned some very important lessons, not least of which was that I could count on my dad in a jam—even if he was not usually proactive in giving things.

I also learned the very important principle of living up to what you say, as well as over delivering and under promising. It also didn't go unnoticed that sometimes, for the sake of family, a matriarch or patriarch will make personal sacrifices to help their offspring. The comfort of knowing your parents are there for you builds trust, love and appreciation. It is akin to the feeling many members of the armed forces know—being confident that someone has your back. Integrity—through action—leads to strong feelings of trust. And trust is the bedrock of any relationship, whether business or personal. People need to know they can count on you—no matter what the relationship you have with them.

There was one more connection with the Concord that underscores the importance of the family dynamic that my parents instilled in me— and it included Grandma Esther.

When I was 11 years old, I had an opportunity to go to an overnight camp. It was an incredible experience—being in a cabin with 11 other kids and a few counselors. The entire ambiance of sports, fun, camaraderie and competition amongst the tribes was exhilarating.

When the next summer rolled around, my father told me, "We can't afford the $500 for camp this year." I was crushed.

My mother took it upon herself—without telling my father—to approach my dad's mother, Grandma Esther, and ask her to help out. Even though Grandma Esther had a very limited budget at the time, she was very close to my mom and I had a special place in her heart. I was named after her youngest son, David, who had died at age 18, a hero in the Marines. My father was not delighted my mother had approached his mom, but she agreed to pay the $500 and I was off to camp.

How does Grandma Esther relate to the Concord? Well, my father used to tell a famous story about his mother. Grandma Esther was not only a very sharp businesswoman, but was a very beautiful woman when she was younger. Before I was born, she had become a widow. Once, she went with some friends to the Catskills, where there were many modest bungalows for her to rent with her friends—they didn't have enough money to stay in a luxurious resort.

As it turned out, an acquaintance who had lived in the same *shtetl* as Grandma back in the old country had come to America and become a very successful businessman. His name was Wanerik, and apparently he had invented some type of hair tonic and made a fortune. When he heard my grandma was in the area, he invited her to join him for dinner and a show at the Concord, where he had a summer residence.

Wanerik sent a limousine to pick up my grandmother. Her friends were agog when they saw it pull up. After my grandmother returned to the bungalow, she was besieged with questions about her experience and Wanerik, himself.

Her response?

"I did not care for him back in the old country, and I don't particularly care for him now."

In my grandmother's world, money was no criteria for her to choose someone to associate with. I believe my father liked to tell this story over and over to illustrate the point. To him, trust and a shared sense of values were much more important than money.

There was one more time in my life where my father was really there for me. About a year before he passed away, we were having business difficulties. The company's cash flow was not sufficient—which is one of the most critical components of being able to properly run a business.

Ever since I had joined my father in the company I had been very concerned about showing my gratitude financially. Early on, we established a pension plan for him. It was something I learned was a good financial tax strategy when I was in law school. And it worked well because Dad was, by nature, a saver.

But when my father learned about the financial problems the company was having, he was as supportive as he could be. He eliminated his salary—without any request to do so. When he did, I had the same feeling I'd had back at the Concord, when he was there for me. I was reminded that I could count on him to the best of his ability, despite never having promised anything.

My dad used to say, "Actions speak louder than words." He lived this mantra every day of his life. And I have found this to be so true in my own life that I've often felt so blessed that he imbued me with this strong sense of responsibility and desire to earn the trust of whomever I'm dealing with through my actions rather than my words.

## *Principle*

# The power of integrity and trust: always under promise and over deliver.

# Epilogue

What are fathers for? Support, transmitting wisdom, guidance, discipline when necessary, and love. This has been my experience. As Dad said, "Good judgment comes from experience; unfortunately, experience comes through bad judgment." I believe that everything happens to us is for a reason. We strive to add meaning to our lives and, in the process, find that elusive meaning.

I have no regrets about my life and relationship with my dad, or for what happened. Instead, I have tried to learn from the things that bothered me growing up and change those things with my own children—including the lack of fun times we spent together or even just the amount of time Dad was accessible. This was one of the goals I have for my relationship with my children. This is not an indictment of my father, who was to a certain extent a product of his environment, which shaped his attitudes. Dad was a child of the Great Depression, and as such was not a big spender. He always had that shadow lurking over him, an uncertainty of where the next meal might come from.

Fortunately, I achieved a modicum of material success early on, benefiting primarily from the opportunity to leverage my dad's resources and ongoing business to enjoy not just the material trappings of life but an ability to leverage my own time so that I had more of it to spend with my family and my passion—playing golf.

My father made very profound contributions to my life, the most important of which were wisdom, support, and the ability to be there for me whenever I needed him. This gave me the confidence to try new things and look for the deeper meaning of what my life was to eventually become. Dad's impact in this regard has been everlasting and led to an ongoing sense of direction and guidance in all the vicissitudes of life.

Dad was human—complex in his inconsistencies and sometimes deprecating in his way of relaying, "Do as I say, not as I do." As I reflect on this, I don't think he was hypocritical. Instead, I believe he hoped for the best in me and all of his children. He wanted us to be armed with the strength and resilience to deal with the ups and downs of life. This was his message of self-sufficiency.

As the years go by, the light of our relationship does not dim. Rather, it burns in an everlasting manner that compelled me to write this story. I hoped to provide some good advice and interesting stories, not just as a legacy for my children, but for the world at large. It pleases me deeply to know that these words came easily and fluently for this book, due to all the time and chance I have had to apply my father's wisdom the best I could.

I have tried to be a good dad, myself, and to pay forward to my children the wisdom and good values my father gave me. One recent experience demonstrated that perhaps some of his sayings penetrated their thought processes.

Recently, I lost my temper at the dinner table and said some inappropriate things about a relative. When my daughter Ashley called me out on this, she gently told me it was not the time or place to have this particular conversation. I admitted my mistake and thought back to my dad saying, "If I make a mistake and someone tells me, say 'thank you and ouch' at the same time for stepping on my toes." This helped me readily rectify the situation, admit my wrongdoing, and want to strive higher to reach the ideals I learned from my dad.

Finally, I want to end this tale by telling Dad, "I love you!"

# About the Author

David Kottler is a national speaker, author, and entrepreneur who combines his legal and business experience with a passion for philanthropy. He earned his law degree from Cleveland State University while helping his family build Decatur Foods, a successful food distribution business that was responsible for introducing numerous retail products to the Cleveland market, including Häagen-Dazs and Ben and Jerry's. Decatur Foods ultimately achieved a 35 percent market share of ice cream sales in Northeast Ohio.

In 1995, David changed careers and became a financial planner, where he was able to pursue his lifelong goal of helping business owners and families effectively transfer wealth and make an impact through philanthropy. Today, through his company, Insurance Doctor™, David leverages outside-the-box thinking to create game-changing results for his clients by using an innovative "True Value" life insurance review process that employs creative buy-and-sell techniques. Over the past few years he has generated millions of dollars in cash and tax benefits for his clients.

David's main passion is philanthropy. He believes there is a great need for education and guidance for high net worth individuals who wish to align life goals with hard earned wealth. David's objective is to collaborate with clients to produce the best financial and philanthropic results for them by enabling them to understand the *why* of planning.

He lives in Cleveland with his wife, Marcela, where they have raised a blended family of nine children and currently have five lovely grandchildren. He is an avid golfer, which has been a lifelong passion.

Contact David Kottler:

http://lifeinsurancedr.com/

(216) 857-0282

DKottler@LifeInsuranceDr.com

dkottler0112@gmail.com